Nature's Inspirations

Rosemarie Cavaney

Published by Rosemarie Cavaney
Email: cavaney@xtra.co.nz

ISBN 0-473-09765-6

Printed by Craig Printing Company Limited,
122 Yarrow Street, PO Box 99, Invercargill, New Zealand.
Email: sales@craigprint.co.nz   Website: www.craigprint.co.nz
2003-70430

Acknowlegements

To my parents: for the love you gave and peace that you brought to our lives. As spirit bodies you continue to provide meaning to my life.

To my dear husband Neil: for your patience, love and understanding. Thank you also for the use of your beautiful photographs on Goals, Peace, Values and Xenial.

A very special thanks to Beverley: for your very helpful comments and editing; and to Diane for your wonderful visualisation of the cover's requirements.

Special thanks to my sons and their families: for your enthusiasm and encouragement.

To my friends for your guidance and inspiration: for me to name each and every one there may be a disappointment for any one I miss, so this is written to you all.

Helping each other is what life is all about.

To each and everyone – thank you. This book has taken a long time to get published, but your encouragement has helped throughout.

CONTENTS

PHOTOGRAPHS

Introduction

I have always loved the beauty of nature. I grew up in Opunake, Taranaki, New Zealand where we had Mount Taranaki on the horizon (although we always knew it as Mount Egmont) and the Tasman Sea on our doorstep. Summer days were spent swimming in the Waiaua River or in the sea, surfing the waves as their power spun us towards the shore. On winter days the mountain drew us for picnics when Dad could take the time off. I walked the bush tracks and also around the local lake, and biked along country roads feeling the wind in my face, enjoying the peace.

I spent many happy times with the Maori Youth Group and learnt from them the joy of *'spirit'* through their song and poi dance.

My mother loved poetry and made a book for each of us using her collections and written in her beautiful script then decorated with pictures of gardens, flowers and birds. Something special I will always cherish.
These are the memories I treasure from my childhood.

Life has not always been easy since my early teens. There have been many occasions for me to think about its meaning. I started writing poems in 1980 when I faced yet another challenge in my life and I felt the need to write down my thoughts, feelings and emotions to help me through the tough times. I have always turned to nature for healing, using the power of the sea, the peace amongst the bush and the strength of the trees.

Southland, where I live now, provides the most amazing opportunities to feel '*spirit*'. It is found everywhere here, in the people and the countryside and it inspired me to put my thoughts to paper so that others might also find solace through '*Nature's Inspirations*'. Many of the photographs have been taken around this region, some from other parts of New Zealand, and there are three from Australia.

Rosemarie Cavaney

Look at your surroundings. Feel the vibrations from nature

Awakening

See the dawn arising
God's fingers warm the earth
The rays of light beam down upon
Each tiny leaf for growth

Open wide your arms
Embrace the glow within
Smile upon the new day
Don't let the light grow dim

Step forward to the future
Surround yourself with love
Happy thoughts to fill the mind
Awakened from above

Queens Park

Early morning awakening in Queens Park, Invercargill

Life is a wondrous thing and I open my heart to celebrate it

Feral Goose "Gavin"

The people of Queenstown have adopted and named
this goose with the beautiful wings seen floating on
Lake Wakatipu, Queenstown

Surround yourself with unconditional love

Beauty

He glides along the lake
Ruffled feathers on his wing
Much like a ballet dancer
Across the stage floating

His beauty is portrayed
In feathers fluffed at will
Then we hear him calling
To our ears, it is no trill

For his mate the call is bidding
And his beauty will bestow
A courtship made in heaven
Friends through life they'll grow

The small things are no flaws
When a partnership begins
Everything is beautiful
And it's always love that wins

Communication

I hear no sound
Yet there you are
Your eye meets mine
I know your needs
Here, take these crumbs to feed

No line between us
Just our minds
You do not speak
I need no words
You communicate your need

There are many other ways
A smile, a touch
Or use of voice
Clear communication
Helping humans to succeed

Black Beaked Gull

This black beaked gull flies beside the steamer 'Earnslaw'.
Lake Wakatipu, Queenstown

A smile is a curve that can set a lot of things straight

The Remarkables

The Remarkables, a mountain range near
Queenstown, Central Otago

Let not the word 'hate' enter your vocabulary

Disappearance

Such a little bit of snow
Where did it all go?
It melted away with the sun

Like our own tales of woe
Heartache and sorrow
Need warmth for joy to come

Energy

The wave gets its energy
From the depth of the sea
It wells up with power
Unseen strength rolling in
Released on the shore

The tide gets its energy
From the moon up above
Pulling it higher and higher
At full moon in a spin
Then next month once more

We get our energy
From strength grown inside
Positive thoughts are our saviour
They're built from within
Refuel o'er and o'er

The Rocks

Riverton/Aparima is the 'Riviera' of the South
and located on the coast near Invercargill.
Stewart Island/Rakiura is in the background

I replace stress with calming thoughts

Skies over Foveaux Strait

Paua hue sky at Riverton/Aparima, Southland
The paua is the New Zealand abalone and the
shell's colour comes from its surroundings.

I feel self-confident from the inside out

18

Feelings

Stand and look around you
Nature's colours bring emotion
To enrich your soul within

It may be with a touch
Or a flourish caught by eye
That creates a stir inside

You are conscious of vibration
Sent by all that is around
Pause a moment, take it in

The excitement brings pleasure
Your senses are renewed
You and nature side by side

Goals

Imagine from whence I came
Mountains, valleys, tributaries named
Then down with a whoosh I fall to a pool
And rest awhile in the shade and the cool

Life's like that, all the time rushing through
Pathways well trodden to goals set anew
Finally reached when all come together
Then time left to ponder and dream of forever.

Millaa Millaa Falls

Millaa Millaa Falls are between Cairns and the
Atherton Tablelands, Queensland

Working hard is a cure for many things,
because there is no time to dwell on trivialities

Daybreak January 1st 2000

Daybreak of the new Millennium 6a.m.
Wanganui

Receive love and intimacy willingly

Healing

The sunrise heralds the new Millennium
It is the Age of Aquarius
Let peace come upon this earth
It is in my light for all to see
Take time to listen to my voice
It is in the song of the birds
Take time to feel my warmth
It is in the rays of the sun

Heal yourself for you have the means
It is in your laughter
Listen to the trill and beat
It is in your music
Lighten your burden as each day dawns
It is there for you

You are now one with yourself
I am all around you
I am nature
I am here to heal
Use me lovingly

Inspiration

Let the scene infuse
Inspiration is around
Divine influence

Encourage others
You be an inspiration
For them to follow

(Haiku is Japanese poetry in three lines of 5, 7, 5, syllables)

Blue Lake

This lake resulted from sluicing for gold,
St Bathans, Central Otago

Know yourself and all will be made known to you

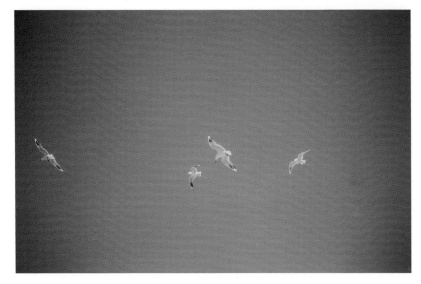

Gulls

Black beaked gulls soaring high above Lake Wakatipu,
Central Otago

Laugh and the world laughs with you

Joy

With joy we will fly
Our mood uplifting
It puts us on high
Like birds on the wing

What makes us this way?
True friends we hold dear
Who bring laughter each day
And send forth good cheer

For joy is a feeling
That you shouldn't keep
Spread it with smiles
To all whom you meet

Kinship

Hills and mountains
Pastures and sky
Grasses and trees
Sheep grazing by

In tune with each other
As one with the land
This typical bond
Found in New Zealand

Neighbours and brothers
Cultures entwine
Living in unison
Hands holding thine

Te Wahi Pounamu World Heritage Region

This was taken near the Makarora Valley,
in the Te Wahi Pounamu Region,
South West New Zealand.
This is a World Heritage Area.
Part of the Southern Alps form the background.

Live with love in your hearts

Kowhai Park

The autumn leaves have carpeted the verge
along the Whanganui River, Wanganui

Move to vibrations to ease your mind tensions will roll away

Letting Go

What is autumn, but a breeze
Denuding all the splendid trees
Carpeting ground beneath with leaves

Time to walk along the road
Breathing, feeling, nature's mode
Ridding minds of heavy load

Doesn't it feel good letting go?
Of all our toils and woe
Preparing selves to within grow

Magic

There is magic in the air
You can feel it everywhere

Just look around and you will seize
A brand new sight with every breeze

Daytime pictures in the sky
Night time stars that twinkle high

A rush of wind another sight
Our eyes receive the image bright

Wonder, greatness, joy and fun
Magic made for everyone

Clouds

Cloud formation, Central Otago

Visualize where you want to be

Hoar Frost

Hoar frosts in Alexandra provide incredible landscapes
in this Central Otago region

Doubt is a pain too lonely to know that Faith is his twin brother

Naiveté

Born to give us pleasure
Limbs spread to catch the sun
Clothed from spring to autumn
Yet, here, naked branches
Naïve to cold it seems
Winters icy crystals sprung

The beauty of our children
Awareness unreserved
Naturally unimpeded
Thoughts and actions simple
Naïve to learned fear
Their minds are unrestrained

Openness

Open fields
Stretching to beyond
Mountain peaks
Reaching to the sky
Flowers, colourful, in full bloom

What a joy
To see no flaws
No hidden attributes
For they're on show
Shouldn't this be
How we show ourselves?

Overlooking Lake Hayes

The photo was taken on the roadside travelling from
Arrowtown towards the main
Queenstown – Cromwell highway.
The lupin flowers are in full bloom in early summer.

Simplify your life and its pathway will open to you

Tropical Rainforest Walkway

A platform in the treetops of the tropical rain forest,
Kuranda, Queensland

I am calm whether or not things are going my way

Peace

From treetops tall
The mist abounds
The rain has cleared the air

The platform waits
For trodden feet
Of persons walking there

No sounds are heard
All that is found
Is Peace resounding clear

Quality

This house has social status
Elegantly poised in manicured grounds
Groomed par excellence
Showing quality profound

For the nature that surrounds it
Makes this house just what it is
Groomed with love and affection
Comes superior finesse

Surround yourself with love
Let attributes come forth
Build upon your character
To Quality – give birth

Anderson Park Art Gallery

Anderson Park Art Gallery is a Georgian-styled residence
in Anderson Park, Invercargill

Life is for living, for giving and receiving. Balance it out

Maple Glen Gardens

This black swan is mirrored on one of the lakes
at Maple Glen Gardens in Wyndham, Southland.
These gardens are a blaze of colour all year.
Colourful Australian birds fly freely in the treetops

I live a positive and loving life

42

Reflections

A mirror image
The grace and beauty
Of the swan
Reflected in
Supreme imitation
No parody here

Reflect yourselves
Emotions to portray
What others see
Mirrored warmth
Will then return
To linger near

Strength

The redwood stands
In forest green
Reaching skyward
Tall, serene

Sit next to them
And rest at length
Let body draw
Upon their strength

Californian Redwoods

The Californian redwood forest at
Mount Bruce Native Bird Sanctuary in the
Wairarapa region of the North Island, NZ

Meditate to bring peace to thee

Rainforest Stream

Tropical rainforest near Cape Tribulation,
Queensland, Australia

I experience and sense inner peace

Tranquillity

It is here the running water
Flows out to the sea
Feeding natures garden
Bringing peace to thee

Look into this haven
Feel yourself grow calm
Let the running water
Soothe and then embalm

Now you are replenished
Tension leaves your face
Tranquillity is all around
In this blessed place

Unity

Ferns belong
Within the native bush
No clash with other flora
All is one with the bush

We belong
Within our circle of friends
No clash with foe or hatred
All is one with the circle

You belong
Within this body given
No clash with fear or anger
All is one within you

Blechnum sp.

One of the varieties of ferns found
on the Glory Track, Bluff.

I make decisions systematically and appropriately

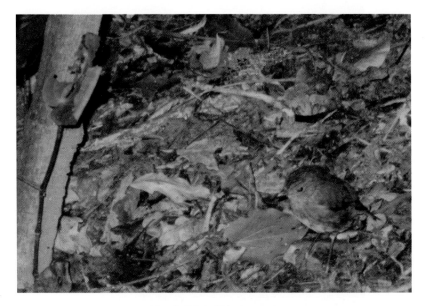

North Island Toutouwai

This is a female North Island Black Robin.
The species is threatened and has been brought
to Kapiti Island for protection.

Everything in creation is harmonious.
It's only man who has tried to spoil it —
Betty Shine "Mind Waves"

Values

Value to our country
Are our native birds
Living, flying free
Unbound with no protection
Endangered some may be
Survival ensured on Kapiti

Value to our friendship
Are agreements being filled
Living, loving be
Unbound excellence show forth
Endanger none to thee
Survival for humanity

Winners

These beautiful blooms
Excel in size, shape and hue
They've been tended and nurtured
Encouraged, they grew

For people to partake
And aim for their best
There is added enjoyment
When the prize is a first

If we go throughout life
Little goals to pursue
Then we will always be winners
As each step comes true

First Prize Dahlias

First prize dahlias, National Dahlia Society of NZ
Wanganui 2000

Enjoy your life and your patience will be rewarded

Thistle Hosting Bees

Busy bees collecting pollen from thistle flower

Unselfish love is the greatest healer of them all

Xenial

Thistle hosting bees
Welcome guests tho' brief their stay
One with each other

Their life sustained
Bees to collect the pollen
Plant propagation

Friends we all need
Welcoming them to our home
Hospitality

Parents to be there
Providing love and sharing
For security

Youth

Kids newly born
Innocent display
On face smile is worn
They greet each new day

Diamonds feel rough
When they are new
Gentle polish brings tough
Character through

Youth to us all
Is the child within
No guilt to recall
Curiosity's a whim

Nurtured to stay
Forever young
For this will portray
Youth's wonders unsung

Kids in Spring

Springtime in New Zealand is a time for the birth of our animals,
so we enjoy their youth and playfulness

Always 'I can!,' never 'I can't'

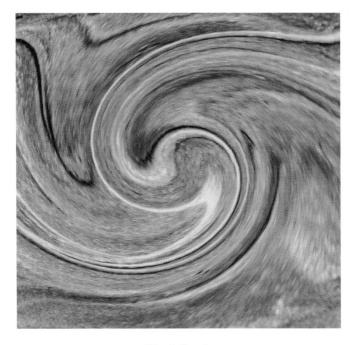

Black Sand

Digital image of water art from a photo
of the black iron sands at Opunake Beach, Taranaki

I recognize and acknowledge my mental powers

Zeal

Whirling
Motion
Art in the sand
Energy
Vibration
Movement at hand

Anger
Passion
Part of our zeal
Ardour
Enthusiasm
Emotions we feel

Strength
Abundance
Love felt inside
Warmth
Desire
In hearts reside

Breathe Nature

Sit yourself down
Take three deep breaths
Relax with no frown
Free thoughts from the depths

Put pen to paper
Scribe all that you feel
You'll look at them later
Their meaning will reveal

When all's said and done
Wait a minute or two
Your mind waves have spun
Now Peace comes to you

Enjoy Nature
Live life

Early morning mist at the pond,
Queens Park, Invercargill